WALKING BAREFOOT IN THE GLASSBLOWERS MUSEUM

Also by Ellyn Maybe:

The Cowardice of Amnesia (2.13.61)

WALKING BAREFOOT IN THE GLASSBLOWERS MUSEUM

ELLYN MAYBE

Manic D Press
San Francisco

Thanks and appreciation to Jen Joseph and Manic D Press, my mom, my grandma Anne, my sister Sherryl, Ron Maxson, Jeff McDaniel, Bernard Goldberg, S.A. Griffin, Ryan Oba and Naomi Weiss, and the benevolence of the poetry community.

The author wishes to acknowledge the following publications and anthologies in which some of these poems originally appeared: *The Ellyn Maybe Coloring Book* (Sacred Beverage Press); *Poetry Slam: The Art of Competitive Poetry* (Manic D Press); *Sic (Vice & Verse)*; *Storie*; *Twisted Cadillac* (Sacred Beverage Press); *Another City: Writing From Los Angeles* (City Lights); *Storie*; and *Short Fuse: An Anthology of Global Fusion Poetry* (Rattapallax Press).

Published with the generous assistance of the California Arts Council.

Cover design: Scott Idleman/Blink

Library of Congress Cataloging-in-Publication Data

Maybe, Ellyn.
 Walking barefoot in the glassblowers museum / Ellyn Maybe.
  p. cm.
 ISBN 0-916397-80-7 (alk. paper)
 1. Los Angeles (Calif.)—Poetry. 2. Women artists—Poetry. I. Title.

PS3563.A9425 W35 2002
811'.54—dc21
                    2002009688

Contents

BEING AN ARTIST

Being an artist
    means the recession will always be there
    and has always been here
    while you sit not writing screenplays
    not taking meetings
    just writing love letters to Van Gogh's beard
    not wearing a watch
    not caring who's on the cover of *People* magazine
Being an artist
    means you might sleep awfully late
    you might choose totally different things
    as the four major food groups
Being an artist
    might mean you feel depressed and make others feel
    distressed when they are near you
Being an artist
    means you've probably memorized the aisles
    at the 99 cent store
    you probably have a $6 service charge each month
    for low funds in your checking account
Being an artist
    means you don't feel you have the right to remain silent
Being an artist
    might make people think you're on drugs
Being an artist
    means people think your closet is full of turtlenecks and
    mood rings
    people assume you play harmonica
    people assume you know all the words to every song
    released in the 1960s
Being an artist
    means you do

Being an artist
	means serenity, intensity, sometimes simultaneously
Being an artist
	means you have the power of civil disobedience on the tip
	of your tongue
Being an artist
	means shrinking tie-dyed tee-shirts 'cause you were
	thinking about a poem and
	didn't notice the washer was on hot water
Being an artist
	is an active verb
	a noun
	a consonant
	an adjective in a world full of chaotic life sentences
Being an artist
	is not necessarily a choice

CHARISMA

He looks like he spreads
    charisma over the ocean of his biceps.

There are preservatives bursting like ribs in Eden.

Been there.
Done that.
The amnesiac sharpens wisdom teeth
    with a sliver of the moon lodged so deep in the finger,
    antiseptic and string
    battle like explorers for territory.
Genius is this verb scattering snowflakes across my heart's winter.

I ignore the wheelbarrow of salt the meteorologist prescribed
    to keep my bones from becoming fossils.
There is a man of letters looking out the windows of envelopes
    squinting at the rain.
There is a word that drowns on the tips of our tongues.
There are boats searching for life-jackets in saliva.
There are beds and breakfasts where the pancake makeup is thick.
Blood is stronger than watercolor.
Guernica lives in the magician's pillowcase.
When did disappearance become the national cuisine?
Who sponsored all those coupons?

In our syllable potluck, we make meals of each other.
A couple of adjectives here.
A couple of past participles there.
And we feast, too blurry to notice the expiration date
    has been crossed out 300 times.
Hunger does strange things to the mind.
I have migraines from the clanging utensils demanding nourishment.

Praying to lick the batter off the most compassionate recipes
    that can be found.
There are a million servings of vinegar with grenadine.
It's not a Shirley Temple.
It's not a Roy Rogers.
Could it be the masked elixir?
Get the smelling salts.
My nose has a history of its own.
I detect salmonella or maybe it's an ice cube whirlpooling upstream
    wrapped in an astronomy of starfish.

Charisma leaves burn marks on the oven.
Charisma gets the best seat in the restaurant.
Charisma eats for two.
Charisma puts his Achilles heel in his mouth so often,
    it's a recital of bunion pornography.
Charisma has a pop-up fairy tale powerbook full of appointments
    to blow your self-esteem down with lungs intravenously
    connected to the unabridged edition of *Women's Wear Daily*.
Then he'll suck the marrow of your porridge.

Charisma whispers with all the spinach in the world in his teeth.
Reflect, genuflect and speck.
All can be used in the same sentence.

Charisma by itself is a toothbrush with a single bristle.
In a world of waterpik wannabes, mouthwash sings into the opera
    of my gums, and I vow to turn over a new botany.

But I'm susceptible like a blade of grass at a gathering of concrete.

COFFEEHOUSE CANTATA

Where are the armies?
Who killed a country
and turned a strong man into a baby?
Now comes the rebel.
They are welcome.
I wait in anger and amusement
in my rehearsals for retirement.
                    — Phil Ochs

This man came into the coffeehouse I work at.
I was playing Phil Ochs' *Rehearsals for Retirement.*
I saw his skin pull away.
His nerves so obvious.
His muscles giving in to the tears.
He looked young but wasn't.
He looked old – no laugh lines, only laughed at lines.
He gazed at the cassette player as if to say
     brother, I'm hearing you now.
He saw me sitting there with apples in my hands and
     realized there is history in the instant.

I saw he had been picked on – picked last for sports –
     for everything.
His mom smothered him.
His dad was disappointed he wasn't aggressive.
His uncle was mad he wouldn't steal pills from the hospital
     where he worked as a psychologist.

I almost said that's Phil Ochs but it didn't matter.
When you hear truth or beauty, sometimes it doesn't matter
who says it
     just as long as you hear it.

His mind was full of chess boards and reruns of *Star Trek.*
He wanted to take over the government, but he almost always
does what he's told.
His mom said come in before 10:00 – come in before it's dark.

This man drowns his passions in Ovaltine.
He stays skinny by running around his house,
the carpet creating electricity,
    shocking treatment for a child.
He knows it's a conspiracy.

He's 41.
He's read about the radicals — heard what they do.
He doesn't know who he belongs to.
He knows the Pledge of Allegiance is an awful song.
He used to go into the cloakroom and pull out his eyelashes
when he heard that song.
His parents said ain't our boy some dramatic actor.
He's going to be making us proud.
They took him to a therapist and said can you make him fit in?
The therapist said yes and no.
He was told to live in the hospital.
Live where the morning is the night.
Where the food tastes like cigarettes.

He said what am I doing here?
It's power that's mad.
I just want to live with my songs – with my Mr. Spock ears.
My feelings, oh my feelings.
He said I shouldn't be in here.
They left him alone.
Ignoring him when he expected tenderness.

When he heard of the Indians of All Tribes takeover
    of Alcatraz Island,

he said I danced.
When he heard of man on the moon,
   he said woman has always been there.
When the elections were held every 4 years, he pointed to his heart
   and murmured this.

His parents thought he was weak.
His grandparents thought he had been raised badly.
His teachers thought he was an inappropriate human being,
   that's what his algebra teacher said in 1965.

The girls thought he was cute in a Mister Rogers sort of way.
One girl liked him but she was considered a weirdo
   so he immediately went after her.
They planned demonstrations.
They grew their hair long.
They looked at Triple A books for Canada.
They were fighting the war at home.
They were not going to put on a uniform.
No camouflage.
They couldn't go chameleon.
Wars always found them.
Invisible pieces of soul were torn and blood filled lives
   were right here.
The government sent people away on airplanes
   when they should be in Washington
   putting the president on a plane with mirrors and
   caskets filled with children.

That's what he dreamed about every night he woke up in Vietnam.
Why was he there?
Why didn't he resist?
The high school boys dared him to go.
He needed to seem strong to somebody.

He brought his songs, but his anxiety clogged his ears with screams
    and guilt gave him ulcers.
He couldn't listen to the radio and he couldn't hear the lyrics
    of any songs.
He could only remember how it went.

They passed out voter registration cards to the soldiers.
He took his time.
Ran to a city to get a newspaper that would give clarity
    on the candidates.
He voted, euphoric, happy so happy.
He walked proudly, gladly till he saw a fire in a corner
    of the military land
    and when he saw the smoke, he saw his name.
His ballot and all the other votes were rising in ash.
He saw his name.
When he saw it clearly, he heard the music again.
songs of Phil Ochs
songs of Leonard Cohen
songs of warriors
songs of men and women
songs written right on the spot
when a heartbeat leaves behind something that must be left behind
but not forgotten.

In winter, he came to a room and saw only a peace sign
where before had been only shattered missing pieces.
His face was all faces.
His fear was all fears.
He was all cowboys.
He was all Indians.
He was all prophets.
He was all wicked.
He was all red.
He was all blue.
He felt hungry and full.

He came into the coffeehouse and listened to his history
shoving the clef notes
and the drum into the future.
He was strong, and happy to admit it.
He was vulnerable, and happily celebrated it.

He said on the Vietnam War Memorial, they should have put
each person's name for when one person dies in the war,
we all die a little.

He walked out, the smell of birth on his breath.
He said, we are the poison and the healing.
We are the sword and the bandage.
We are the powerful and the truly powerful.

He whispered sometimes I get scared.
He whispered sometimes I can only whisper.
I said sometimes a whisper is really a scream.
He said come with me.
I said I am with you.

I saw his face in the moon.
I saw his eyes in my mom's wedding picture.
I saw his touch in a Van Gogh painting.

He walked home.
He lived around the corner.
He said, "Mom, it's 9:30, can I go out and look at the stars?
I promise, cross my heart, I'll be in by 10:00."

DESERT GRAIN

It's as if you put 5 pennies in a gumball machine
    and out came grace.
Sometimes vocabulary does the shimmy with humility.
You make parentheses bend over in a choreography worthy
    of Merce Cunningham.
You've learned the capital city of Psyche is empathy.
You are brilliance blended with candor.
You don't act as though you keep a dictionary in your underwear.
There's an astronomy to knowing which way
    the planetarium's beard points tonight.
There's a thermometer sticking out of your hair like a cowlick.
There's a hymn crossing your cheekbones.
There's a sand glass painting with your name on it
and I'd steal a desert grain by grain to give you more time.

GRANDMOTHER HAIR

Grandmother hair is found on my head again.
It happens when I break.
My 27-year-old body grows oldest on top.
It takes stress spelled with 15 s's.
It takes tension with 100 t's.
It takes the absolute opposite of toupee.
My hair is a mood ring for how I feel.

I grew close with my grandparents at an early age.
Shabbat dinners
singing *Hello Dolly* and *West Side Story*
letting Grandma comb my hair
watching basketball games
drinking grape juice instead of wine
having Grandpa threaten to cut my hair with a scissors
    (while I was asleep)
the hippie of Milwaukee.

I got my first grandmother hair the crayola of gray in Manhattan
    while I tried to get housing.
It was a YMHA-YWHA that didn't dig non-conformists.

People every couple of months inevitably say
    "You've got a gray hair."
They put their hands on it ready to pull like I want it gone.

This isn't a Susan Sontag thing or Phil Donahue.
I don't want my hardships removed from my head –
    my mind maybe.
But there is reality like dried leaves on top like whipped cream.
What sundae is complete without it?

Your hair has about as much gray as mine
     but it's your heart where the real gray has lingered.
I want to pull the pain away from your heart and fill it
     with comfort.
You want to pull things beneath my hair.
It's a battle of elders at a young age.
We are too young to have nothing to say to each other.

Anytime I spread myself too thin, I get grandmother hair.
My grandmother has granddaughter hair.
It's hopeful.
It's full of emotional ribbons.

My hair is falling out.
Bombs are going off in my vagina and I'm still a virgin.
No nukes – No kidding.
I lost 3 grandparents in a year and a half.
They don't make maps to get you where they are now.
Memories, thank G-d I have them —
     I never want to have no memories.

I ONCE HUGGED SOMEONE

I once hugged someone thin like you.
I was leaving for good.
This was an occasion.
He could justify hugging me.
I was off to the sand land.
New York hugged New York and became California.
As I hugged him, I felt his bones and realized this hug would
    damage him.
He'd have to show how uncomfortable this made him
    right down to his tendons.
He'd have to make me see we had no chance for passion.
He'd have to convince me good.
He'd have to insult me in some way.
He'd have to play a Doors song – a Marianne Faithful song.
He'd have to have his voice crack a little.
He'd say he'd visit.
He'd say you need a lover.
I said it all with my eyes.
Growing weather in my heart.
Scarecrows stand tall in fields – urban and other parts unknown.
Did I make a mistake leaving such a good platonic friend?

I once hugged someone thin with experience.
New to what was happening.
Intrigued by what was happening.
Unable to travel long enough to travel.
He went home and covered his windows with wallpaper
    that had only the word fear written on it.

I once hugged someone thin but all bones did
    a 4th of July spark in our spin,
      red and white meant the blues.

We threw history books at each other.
Caught between the sun and the moon.
He acted as though I was a paper doll and he was a scissors.

I once hugged someone after I hugged someone.
My arms were still wrapped around the knees of that memory.
He said you've done this before.
He could feel the expression on his face,
    but not the expression on my face.
He was dreaming aloud lying and I was blasted from wounds,
    eager for dreams.

Wary of what people expect of me.
Expectations are the marrow and joy of depression.
I can handle being alone.
I can't handle being alone.
He loves me.
He loves me not.
I've suffocated from not being sent flowers.
I revive by knowing I am flowers when I breathe in a caring way.
I wanted chocolate.
I got thorns dipped in sugar.

Boldly I hug with adrenaline, laughter and luggage.
People squeeze me close and I know, fat as I am,
    they're squeezing fractured particles of all the tenses
    and the senses.
Sometimes I'm water and I leave the hug earlier than the other.
Sometimes I'm neon and initiate the hug.

When I must, I back away.
I charge into loneliness like a bull.
But I am not ready for a matador to gore me.
I am not ready to be a piñata,
    even though I love the ethereal moment
    before everyone begins digging for edible thrills.

People can't be trusted to eat.
They start with your fingers and when you make a fist saying
    give, don't just take,
     they swallow your arm up to the elbow
     and they consider themselves
     absolutely brilliant hunters.

And they all love their style.
And they love to stuff their mouth with red carpets.
They consider themselves royalty and welcome mats
    hang from their ass.
They want you there.
But one can tell that would be a mistake.

And, like any disappointed soul, I can be a contortionist,
    re-enacting your heat with my own hands,
     humming your dependability with a wild horse's snarl.

And, like any disappointed soul,
I can be a clown.
I can be a tightrope walker.
I can be cotton candy wrapped in iron peanut shells.
I can be soda losing its fizz as the freak show changes directions.
I can watch the carny's tongue fall out in promises.
I can see the carny doing his charisma dance.
I can see him dip me.
I can see him wink before he drops me.
I can see him wink before he drops himself.

He thinks he runs things.
When he sees he doesn't, he takes it to another tent.

bye bye

I WAS DRIVING ON THE 405

I was driving on the 405 and saw a police car
   with flashing lights changing lanes
   coming toward me.
I always drive probably a little fast.
I mentally planned traffic school.
8:00 A.M.
Then I saw the car behind me pull off the road into
   the vulnerability of the shoulder.

The police car was after them, not me.

I realized this is how you live.

So close to being harassed.
So close to being beat up.
So close to being called a name.
So close to remembering your memories.
So close.

When I see riots and tear gas, I see our skin separate.
I realize our ancestral humor goes through common longing
   in resistance.
I know the effort you will not make until you are ready
   to accept I am not a war.

KINGDOM OF STRING

There's a kingdom made of string.

Shields composed of novels and nerves held levitating.

The swords are number infinite pencils with bright purple erasers
   that are too scuffed to forget anything.

The horses quote Daniel Berrigan and Ted Berrigan and then dance
   into a Chagall sky.

No horseshoes allowed.
Bare feet it is.

There's a painter reciting Shakespeare.

There's a pie made of laughter and proclamation.

Jousting: the poetry slams of the past tense.

The guard never changes.
No one lets down their guard.
Everyone's cautious and wild simultaneously.

The king always seems to be opening a new thrift store called
   the emperor's new clothes.

He pouts his ego down the eternal runway.

His attitude on tightly like sweat.

He keeps his bassinet full of water
   which he autographs with toothpaste
   leaving a speck clear so he can do his ode to Narcissus.

He feasts on tears of his servants.
He has 9000 people who will tell him what he wants to hear.
He has 8654 people who will never speak to him.
He has 780 people who scream a lost language in their sleep.

He has 50 people who sew devotional sonnets to him.
He has 26 letters to work with.
Cranky consonants
Voluminous vowels

He tears the hair of the alphabet out with a glance and a stanza.

The people call him king behind his back.
What could be worse than to be put on a pedestal never to be
    called "that guy who just happens to run the land"?
The people write anthems as their time is eaten away.

He watches their dreams take on the geography of snakes.

A collective slither creates a shiver in the world.

People try to create a happy face.
They dash off to all the makers of portraits looking for someone
    unscathed.

But as soon as the lips start to go heavenbound,
    there is a metamorphosis
    into Munch's *The Scream* and Munch hasn't even painted it yet.

And Dylan sings "everything is broken."

Musical notes catch the king with water glasses on his eyes.

His bed is made of H_2O.
Liquid alibis.
He feels the 90% of water the body is made of each time he speaks.

Each time he touches my memory, I struggle to swim.

There are so many ladies in waiting.
Waiting for appreciation.
Waiting to be king.
Waiting to be courted by the king.

Waiting to be Joan Baez for Bob Dylan
    before she was ditched in *Don't Look Back*.

Waiting to hold hands and sing folk songs.

Waiting for a world where Phil Ochs and Richard Brautigan
    and so many others don't die like that.

Waiting for the world to catch up to a Van Morrison song.

Waiting for poetry to be the recreational drug of choice.

Waiting for the world record as people stand on each other's heads
    and walk on water by the sheer possibility of faith.

Waiting for the world where people work
    ten minutes a day in a job and 23 hours and 50 minutes
    at whatever they really want to do.

Waiting for a road that is paved with good impressions
    beyond appearance.

The king says get off the stage.
The jester is due any second.
If you are still talking, he might get ideas.
Ever heard of the 100th jester?
Want to be my 23rd wife?

My 8th sage?
My partridge in a pear tree?

I say,
Don't distract me.
Don't charm me with charisma.
Don't ply me with poignancy.

You turn quicker than a book within inches of a windmill.

The king takes out his scroll for many occasions and bellows.

You are earning a degree in procrastination.
You are summa cum laude in stagnancy.
You are a serf to my every whim and
I am a Svengali to my own genitalia.

I look at him wearing a leather jacket toga and a crown of women's
    underwear thrown Tom Jones-like at his metaphors and skin.

He sneers at me with a royal insecure bow.

He rages against the machination of the shy and
        bookworm ball I've become.

He gave me glasses and then expected blind obedience.

He thinks he had the prescription filled
        with myopic one-night desperation
        with bifocals of benediction
        with cataracts of chaos.

I say here try on my monocle.

I've been alone so long I see differently.

I see in one piece of glass more than you see in your glass house.
You're throwing stones at the self-esteem of the ladies who wait.

And then I walk like a chipped headlight into the town
    of 60-watt stained glass vision.

It is time for the hootenanny of delay.
The unrequited confused room of manners.

There is a gathering of people saying the Serenity Prayer
    in tongues.
There is a room of people who are writing as a thesis project:
    Men who are unwilling to acknowledge their creative kindred
    'cause of sexism, looksism, peer pressure, superficial
    bullshit, conditioning, history, TV, fashion magazines,
    cowardice and the women who somehow pathetically
    year after year adore them – not without reservation.

These are women who would walk to Antarctica
    for a smile from their beloved –
    they'd find a way to Saturn for a hug.

They'd traverse to Venus for a conversation that didn't
    end in sulking.

There is a mail art room for the babble that is never sent.
Rambling phrases to clear the mind when it sifts
    in an edgy kaleidoscope.

The stamps grasp a medley of
    Aretha Franklin's *Respect*
    Helen Reddy's *I Am Woman*
    Patti Smith's *Piss Factory*
    and refuse to stick to the envelope.

The stamps say we've been around a long time,
     since hemp was the paper love letters were written upon.

We've seen a lot.
We've been on the letters with the return address.
wish hope denial please need desire crawl loneliness

I shrug and say most people are too fragile for their record players.

Instead of hearing me roar, the walls hear me say
   can I play *Desolation Row*
   followed by *Dress Rehearsal Rag*
   followed by *It's Alright Ma, I'm Only Bleeding*
   followed by *Stuck Inside of Mobile with the Memphis Blues Again*?

I will roar soon – back off.

The stamp.
A Dylan freak with her own fears of abandonment has a flashback
    and trembles with the playing of the lines
      from *Memphis Blues Again*.

"The post office has been stolen and the mailbox is locked."

The stamp is devastated.
Its ink begins to run.
Now you know why stamps need to be wet to stick.

To try to comfort the stamp, I got my mom's copy of
    Pat Boone's *Love Letters in the Sand*.

She giggles a little.
I roar slightly.
Who are we kidding?

Still it helps.

There is so much survival ahead.

I take a look at where I was.
What a place.

Alarm clocks are banned.
No one wants to wake up.
It's dream time in vertical posture.

The layers of pain go deep.

I see a sign "Periodontal Surgery every 2 seconds"
        and for what
beyond flossing…. beyond genetics…. beyond appetite

It turns out the gums begin to bleed from the
        book recommendations stored there
        gnawing, waiting for the moment
        he's willing to listen to what you're willing to share.

Oh for his taken-for-granted stance to be transcended
        into something nourishing.

There are insomniacs at the town of waiting for the miracle.
People who can't sleep for daydreaming of a life of different.

The kings gather across time sharing inside jokes.

Psst
I think she's loved me longer than a decade.
I think she's losing her hair over me.
I think she's going to be alone because of me.

Then they puff up their egos and airbrush their emptiness.

They do 50 minutes of ego calisthenics.
Belittling people jumping jacks.
Verbal abuse sit-ups.
Relay races where they pass the blame.
Creating scapegoats that fill a never-ending stadium.

They won't even dip an itty-bitty toe into the gender pool.
They're wary of diving down that particularly chewy water
        to inspect the damage they've caused.
They show each other scrapbooks and tapes of their glory days
        – play by play –
        of what benevolence that came to pass during their reign.

There's a space on every tape that's blank.
They make a show.
Call the VCR repair company
Why does this always happen?

They go back to their rooms and cry.

Sometimes the lady-in-waiting catches a tear.
The holy beverage offered by the king
        and this can set her back 800 years
        because she breathes him in so deeply
        she forgets to breathe for herself.

She gives him her best asset – her power.

There are magic places where people go to regain their electricity
        when lightning strikes them.

There are brief moments.
Opportunities to dwell in a line of poetry.
To sit under a fruit tree.

There are nooks and crannies in the cranium that are padded and
    filled with mercurochrome for the wounds that no one sees.

People who feel they have to write your name in invisible ink
    in order to keep equilibrium will attempt to keep you from
    finding the chaise lounge in your mind.

They will switch the furniture.

They will make sure the springs are broken and you thirst for more.
They will steal peas from the Jolly Green Giant and sneak
    a multitude of pods under your mattress.

And they will not have a good reason.

They will stammer, they will point fingers.
They will use cynical as a verb and a run-on sentence.

They will never take the word *sorry* and
    dig into a thesaurus for 100 lifetimes.

They will never tell you your poems, your songs, your letters,
    your tears, your roars, your scars
    made them consider the cruelty of their ways.

They will never give you a map and let you draw
    the continent of search and find for your heart
    so they can come to the discovery with a clue.
They will be thrilled you are bringing utensils
    to feed their arrogance.

They may not show up at the picnic except to bring the rain.

A LOLLIPOP IS BORN EVERY MINUTE

He had an experience with a crystal once.
He talks about all the new age white women who think
    if they sleep with him,
        they'll get this
        they'll get that
        they'll become
        they'll be sacred, holy and extremely satisfied.

He's not used to not getting it.
It means sex.
He sees me as an it.
This is a hero 20th Century style.
The great unexplained phenomenon.

He says sex produces bonding.
It's not just physical to him, he gloats,
but he called that stranger ugly
and that woman dykey
and that other one big breasted
and that one a nice piece of ass.

He lives and breathes snake oil.
The people are lost and searching for heroes
    so they mistake shallowness for enlightenment
    as long as the packaging is good.

The more money charged,
The more people follow,
The more rural environment stimulated,
The more bucolic and real.

Gurumania is sweeping the nation under quick cure conditions.

Assumptions are made if he can't go to bed with me.

He says are you a lesbian?
If I am wearing blue, he says are you sad?
If I am laughing at all this,
    he says you just haven't experienced life yet,
    I'll help you get more spiritual - now take off your clothes.

I rub my eyes to see if this is real.
Pedestals are the clunkiest ladders in the world

Lava lamps I've trusted flash in my memory.
His room smelled like money.
His advice smelled like cum.

He's a success on the teach about how to be instant
lama
rama
dama
mama
right now circuit.

It's religion for dollars
Bowling through vulnerabilities
It's another way for genders to fuck each other and think
they're touching the wettest places.

It's the dating game of heroes.

"Simplicity is outdated" that bumpersticker reads on that car.
People sometimes choose going right on doing what they've done
    rather than being right on.

It's so affordable.
Be your own
hero
leader
pied piper
bird
coyote
fish
drugstore
laughter
singer
cook
poet
friend
book
dancer
sky
air fire music water

and see in everything...

       everything

MANHATTAN

How high everything must have looked.
3 years old in Manhattan.
I imagine your parents ate shredded wheat.
Would they understand you as you grew tall as a stack
    of Joyce Carol Oates books?

3 and counting ellipses.
3 and libraries more important than toy cars.

I bet you saw those Chagall windows at Lincoln Center.
Or Frank O'Hara composing *Lunch Poems* on 53rd St.

At 3 were you already old?
The past biting your heels.

It must have been weird going back to Stockton.
Leaving corned beef for tongue tied.

It must have been hard to leave the yellowest taxis
    and the orangest sun.

It must have been hard to grow up a New York Jew
    without a New York.

Malamud, Singer, Bellow
Paley, Ozick, Aleichem
Potok, Kafka, Howe

Our baseball team of choice.

Your Stockton – 3000 miles away from a good egg cream.
My Milwaukee – 2000 miles away from Papaya King.

Both so far from Second Avenue.

There must have been tons of kids like us.
Wearing glasses at two.
Reading anything from *Curious George* to George Bernard Shaw.
Looking at the world with big brown eyes.
The world squinting back.

na na na na na
It won't be easy.
na na na na na
Kindreds don't grow on trees.

I think I heard a noise when your childhood fell.
The world is full of upended trees.

Lucky ones pull pulp from the citrus of eucalyptus
        and make an alphabet.

Our apartments, bookmobiles.
Spines upon spines hold up the world.
As DSL is to them, D.H. Lawrence is to us.

We might not have met.
Bibliophiles wear solitude with crushed velvet.

When you left Manhattan, you let some bread crumbs
        fall from your pocket.
Finding them, I memorized the places where hummingbirds go.

Years later, I left a marble rolling away from the pack
        as though it had translucent wings.

MYTH

I wanted to feel the music of your shoulders.
Watch the tension of CD turn to 8-track.
I read your nonfiction — if that's not a crush, what is?

You live twenty years away from Richie Havens
    tuning up at a cafe.
I watch the liner notes of your wrists like a fortune teller.
Jerome Robbins choreographs your neighborhood
    with a pale peony.

I heard there's a tree in Washington Square Park dripping
    with handcuffs and a noose.
Phil Ochs sings of the cobwebs of contradiction.
Did you ever wear sandals?
Did you hold a megaphone?
When did you start wearing cufflinks?
When's the last time you played a Fugs song?
When's the last time you kissed a girl who memorized
    Bob Dylan's bootleg releases?
When's the last time you used groovy as a verb?
When's the last time you hummed a Rodgers & Hart song?
When's the last time you went to Kim's Video and rented *Hair*?

How many roads fork into most traveled?
The asphalt is pinstriped.
One-quarter of the time I don't know what decade I'm in.

I watched you watch the parade.
I'm the one who whispered in your ear
    the Army / McCarthy hearings aren't available on DVD.
I'm in the park feeding the pigeons bread and circuses.

Come midnight, I watch Michelangelo
    leaning out of a helicopter,
    he has quite an eye for astronomy.

Every night, Lord Buckley leaves Cafe Wha.
Every night Walt Whitman & Allen Ginsberg fly like Chagall
    above your window.
One night I tagged along with my flailing trampoline.
I tried to visit you like Frank O'Hara's sun.
You drew the blinds.
You took away my yellow.

Suddenly a confetti of tangerines fell from the sky,
    labeled hand-picked by Icarus.
I ate till I was sticky.

98%

I'm 98% sure if I got a lobotomy and plastic surgery,
    he'd be in love with me.

I'm 76% definite if I read less books and
    watched commercials for tips,
        he'd be devoted and true.

I'm 110% positive he uses 500 times
    the recommended daily allowance
        of conditioning.

I took a tweezer and removed one layer of my cornea
    and asked him to see things
        from even the slightest bit my point of view.

He put my vision in a rabbit's hat and pulled out a scapegoat.

He put on a mask coated in sugar and salt swiveling to breathe
    the taste buds of what and who were acceptable.

And who was eating buttons and taking on
    the language of bleating,
        learning extra choruses of *Old Grogan's Goat.*

He turned around and faced me and I said
    have a plate of French fries,
        you have enough salt to create an ocean in your path.

He ran and became rock candy as he got closer.

I said it would be just as well you get a wind machine
    to blow your guilt around.

He ran under the weight of memory.
His feet were 80 feet in the direction of pain.
His memories never moved a muscle.

He said
        dose me with some amnesia.
        give me a bong of dissipation.
        let me thaw out.

I said the clocks have faith in you.
The grandmother clocks are pinching your cheeks.

The cuckoo says let me soar like a peace dove.
Harold Lloyd holds hands with the middle hand of a city tugging
        on the brain of Salvador Dali.

Alarm clocks
Easy over.

Time is like an audiotape on an individual tape recorder.
For some it moves like 1000 trips around Venus
        and nine No Loitering signs ignored per hour.

And for others,
        one memory is stretched like taffy on the roof of the psyche.

And the circus is encrusted in quicksand
        though there's carbonated feelings on the ground
                making it look like liquid smooth traveling.

And the history of the trapeze rope can be exchanged for a net.
But being wrapped in net enough times has the resemblance
        of a straightjacket.

The world is sticky with perfume masquerading as wisdom
        with cologne impersonating benevolence,
        with faces being mistaken for souls.

He said,
        enough
        get off your high horse
        your horse is 100,000 feet tall
        I don't like what your saddle has to say.

You think your reins are made of truth.
I don't have to deal with you
I have a full deck
        and you are part joker
        part queen of hearts
        and part too ethereal to hold.

I watched him run to the assembly line
        looking for predictable packaging,
        groveling at the hem of an encyclopedia
        made of invisible ink,
        a dictionary written in double talk.

He breathed heavily and said
        I'll carry a conversation with you
        when you can't hold up your end

He put a down-payment on a megaphone
        to sit above the cage marked scapegoat.

Don't feed the scapegoat
Let her eat her pride.

Somebody opened the zoo one night.
Somebody let the light in by pawing the gauze
　　off the way things are
Somebody twirled

I ran to you like Tigger.
So enthusiastic.
So unbeknownst to common sense.
Waiting for you to tear up every business card you ever sent.
Recommending a good place to lose my eccentricity
　　and strange itinerary.

And you threw insults
　　like confetti
　　like steel
　　like permanence

And you celebrated the infinity of your irrationality.

And you gave me a kazoo.

You told me I'd need music to survive the damage.

And you said I take things too seriously,
　　didn't I know what a grain of salt was,
　　did I have to become Blake
　　finding eternity in every damn thing?

I said hang on, please don't pass the salt
　　and please don't pass the sand.

My mouth tastes of boats you've sunk.
My eyes are like oars trying to move across these waters
　　and you sit like an iceberg holding a candle,
　　an askew grasp of liberty just wishes away.

I took my thermometer and said,
　　we get to play the Weather Channel for each other
　　we get to be precipitation, snow, hail,
　　meteor shower, fog, sun, rain,
　　eclipse, thunder, lightning

He said I don't get cable.

PICASSO

I found a year that likes my body.
    1921
girl sitting on a rock
Picasso painted a woman with my thighs.

Walking around the museum,
    it hit me how Rubenesque
    is not just some word
    for someone who likes corned beef

There I was
    naked on the edge of something
    overlooking water
    or was it salt?

It was weird.
Nobody was screaming *fat chick* at the frame.
Nobody was making grieving sounds
    but the girl in the painting looked sad
    as though she knew
    new eras were smudging
    a forced liposuction
    with rough acrylic

The caption said
    girl sitting on rock

Not woman who uses food to help cope
    for the lack of empathy in her sphere.

Not the gyms are closed and there are
    better muscles to develop.

Not girl one calorie away from suicide.

Just flesh on a rock.

Her eyes dripping question marks onto
    girl looking into a mirror

The vibrancy.
The need to chew the ice cubism
    till the teeth bleed.
The colors so deep
    they look wet.

The museum guards watch me tentatively.

I lean into the paintings.
I veer to the outside to find out what Picasso
    called each work.

I like titles.
Their vocabulary of oil.

The girl on the rock whispered to me

go girl

I love museums.
Call me old-fashioned but I like face to face conversations.

RANTING GIDGET'S SOCIALLY CONSCIOUS NAVEL

Somebody dared me to write a nature poem,
    a valentine to hiccup trees and grizzly bear salad.
So I woke up, put four herbal teaspoons of lettuce in the museum,
    searched for a thousand words that were worth a picture,
    asked my golf-playing goldfish to say cheese, and put
    on my hiked up khaki bra around my Audubon Society,
    Robert Frost sanctioned breasts.

Los Angeles is a city where the heartburn and ulcers have agents
    and glassblowers pose with Windex.

I like Sunset Boulevard because an old man told me once
    what came first,
    the grape, the raisin or the ocean?

When it's three in the morning
    and the hookers have taken Mr. Easy
    into the cinnamon and pepper hotels, I drive around.
The billboard is still selling Neil Diamond in *The Jazz Singer*
    and I put my leg up on the counter of the International
    House of Pancakes and make them serve me granola and
    other fine a cappella substitutions.

I get arrested for disturbing the batter and lard nutrition squad,
    but this could only happen in a city such as this.

I'd be happy eating buffalo and seeing where the deer
    and the antelope play,
    but now it's all metal swing set in two feet of concreted
    suburbia with rhinestone chimney.

This land was stolen by post office wall dweller Columbus and
    his toothpick boats, Nina, Pinta and Santa Maria.

Mr. Constantly-Up-to-His-Neck-in-Paper-B-52's works for the
    defense corporate way of peace.
The company ladder is just staircases of yarn. Still,
just to be safe, he builds a bomb shelter underneath his property,
    and mows his lawn Saturdays and feels guilty if he doesn't.

I went on looking for a nature poem.
I saw a man beating his dog for bringing in the wrong newspaper.
He wanted the *New York Times* and the dog brought
    in the *Harmonica Press-Telegram*.

A little girl in high heels brings her childhood for the world to burp.
She's seven and wears a necklace that says #1 Mommy.

Norman Rockwell is surrealism.
Ozzie and Harriet are advertisement.
Human billboards
Salvador Dali
Picasso
Mayakovsky
Tell it like it is.

Shoes are only a dream for one-third of the planet.
Cats don't run up trees anymore – the trees are horizontal.
The rainforests are controlled by 1000 Paul Bunyan comic strip
    wannabes.

People grow up on westerns.
Take a look at the way this society treats Native Americans.
John Wayne wears the eternal ultimate bolo tie – sort of a T.V. Hitler
    and Hitler was an art student whose blue period turned
    into blue eyes
    and then into blood.

We watched so many holocausts the same way we watch
    dance contests,
        thinking it's all just bodies under stress.

Patriots with electric dollar bills for teeth manufacture Rolls Royce
    dashboards that tell us the state bird of Delaware,
        but we shrug and can't afford bus fare
    most of the time.

I want to find a tree with rings like hulahoops –
    old and a stream of fish nearby.
I also want to find a bootleg of Bob Dylan doing
    the collected reggae hits of Barry Manilow.

I'm not easy to please.
My welcome mat says maybe
    and nature poems aren't just about hermits.
It's about change and reckless turpentine in underwater murals.

We're a third world country with 58 channels to choose from –
    America in blur.
We have children with pot-bellied malnutrition.
We have luxuries we think we need.

Teenagers walk into stores with American Express cards
    in their own nicknames,
and take credit to its limit saying we grow up with so much
    and so little we'd die for or at least
        get grounded a whole month for.

Butterflies are kept under lock and wing-printed
    'cause they're planet angels and
        only a few are left.
People wear sunglasses when around one
    out of respect for the colors.

Out of shape eyes titter at such maudlin ass-kissing of
        a type of eclipse, something rare,
        could be scrapbooked for money,
        too self-conscious to mate.

Synthesizers haven't quite mastered a bird's chirp.
And as long as one dog still has the power to wake up the
        neighborhood with barks and morning tonsillitis
And one ground hog sees his shadow and realizes
        the government is nothing but
        shadows in a checkerboard game – we king or we don't
They cheat by the rules and also by not the rules – the first rule is
        there are only exceptions and action comes before passive
        in the dictionary.
Passion plus action is impact.

Hey, I'm no saint.
I curse at shit on a car just washed, but I know that bird
        has just been in a piano bar
        whistling some obscure Strawberry Alarm Clock song
        and had to be in the Bay Area in 50 minutes for a
        benefit concert freeing neon and horseshoes,
        no toilet paper as he flew off and couldn't hold it.

So Woodstock owes me one.
So jumpsuits are coming back.
So I'm not Henry David Thoreau.
And I actually find myself liking
        making left turns on Sunset Boulevard.

ROPE BURNS OF A TRAPEZE ARTIST

Monday
Slapped a mosquito off my wrist.
Brushed my back teeth.

Tuesday
Bought Ajax.
Clogged my sink with mobiles of snakes.

Wednesday
Got up.

Thursday
Opened all mail addressed to occupant.
It was for you.

Friday
Took a number at the all-night bakery.
Planned my wedding.
Planned my suicide.
Coordinated the rabbi to please read the right speech.

Saturday
Ate Jell-O.

Sunday
Put on a swimsuit.

Monday
Checked my pulse.

Tuesday
Still alive.
Cleaned up and watched public television.

Wednesday
Winked at a head of lettuce.

Thursday
Gave myself a surprise party.
Showed up an hour late to make it real authentic.

Friday
Purchased a futon.
Picked out curtains.
Stole a mood ring.
Felt sad and gave it back.

Saturday
Threw ocean at the sand.

Sunday
Met a gypsy.
She introduced me to her brother.
He gave me a mood ring.
We danced.

Monday
Bet on the horses.
People placed anyway.

Tuesday
Faced the mirror.
Sold the mirror.

Wednesday
Kept the mood ring.

SALT

Salt is a verb to the foaming mouth
    record jackets buzzed through my fingers
    in rooms of hummingbird breath and bongs
    twister and love beads stringing
    one decade to the next.

Mood rings and their enormous jewels loom large from the
    walls' hands.

Someone has been sitting crosslegged-campstyle on the carpet
    for centuries
guessing how many patchouli marbles it takes to reinvent
    the weevil.

I look in the mirror and see an accordion
    curling and stretching
    crunched and open yet again.

Somebody is building an ashram in the sand.

Somebody is wearing boots with liquid paper in the heel
    to erase their past.

Amidst this, somebody dreams of kissing
    a 45 record twirling
    their courage escaping into a corner of their mouth
    like an animated movie made of saliva.

Mood lighting pulls volcanoes apart for its shine.

The musicologist pulls a stethoscope out of his tonsils
and asks the liner notes to lay back and remember the
screaming and the struggle when mommy
brought home the compact disc.

Take two proverbs and call me in the mourning.

In rooms full of clay and card decks, epiphanies are refrigerated
in the wait for a sweeter universe, a more edible oxygen.

There is a room where behind the Michael Bolton collection is a
Vanilla Ice boxed set.

There are people who can have the telescope placed against
their foreheads but their constellations have gone.

There are rooms where once there were fireflies
and now there is Raid.

The residue of a room that has had the music removed is a cage
with periodontal grief where once had been teeth.

Sometimes I sing along to my Leonard Cohen records
at the time the night is the darkest,
my version of love thy neighbor.

When I sat in rooms and the turntables turned
the speed of light on me, I tried not to blink.

With one cornea in each century, I saw what was coming.

I listened intently as record after record found a history of
who will eat
and who will be eaten.

I wanted to jump into the grooves and caress the makers
        of the music, lie in the needles' path,
        let the holes be filled with gravel and soil to build stronger
        roads and gardens full of rare birds.

There are very few people I can call when there are murals on
        my ceiling telling me Michelangelo lives there too.

In my room, I play myself records.

I play them a little loud to try to let them sing a little
        on the tip of my tongue
        like a secular wafer in a room where the water is rising
        and the seaweed is giving itself an anthem and a throne.

SHOE

I'm looking for my soulmate.
What do I find here?
Eternal supply of heels.

SUNSET BOULEVARD DEMANDS

Sunset Boulevard demands to be watched like a circus
    screeching check me out.
I know your royalty jaywalks across the lemon mannequins
    who are never in when the display windows crumble from
    too much light or Rod Serling wonders why the editors at
    Billboard never noticed…

There is a difference between hearing a show with the bouncer
    wondering if you're someone who's gonna rush into the
    club without a ticket and sing *O Solo Mio* obscuring the
    between set precious so warm version of *Behind the Wheel*
    by Depeche "I'm very sad and I wear salt except for that
    I'm nude" Mode.

The show cost $12.50.
It was $11.50 more than what I had.
I had wanted to bring a couple cans of food in lieu of paper
    with presidents stamped on around paraphrased one-liners
    about liberty, the last cans of food I had given to a
    Native American food bank.

I asked the guy working the door if I could hang out – listen.
He said yes, but from outside.

The door remained ajar.

I heard the last minute trendy chat of a crowd when the
    piped-in music is brought down and the bang takes the stage.
    Last minute talk on finals and where do you get cheap
    beads without going to Mardi Gras, and when is Love and
    Rockets gonna play on the space shuttle?
Where is Poorman Dude and when will K.E.D.G. come back?

Then I heard Bryan Harvey and Johnny Hott rush with their
    tribe of two, their syncopated devilish innocence with the
    possibility of grandchildren and secret languages made for
    those tears in my eyes.

I asked the bouncer who's always named Swen or Kneebone if
    I could please go in a second and see the stage.
I said I'd be right back library card honor.
He said yes.
So I looked and there was Johnny Hott
    looking so Johnny come lately
    and see this is it.
I cannot believe the way he plays drums
    and then kisses those mandolins
    and just when I thought I can't take it no more,
    he takes out a washboard
    and puts it through the cycle.
    Dry
    Rinse
    Permanent press

If this was menopause, this was everything.
I felt great.
I danced and tall people didn't care when I pushed them aside
    for another angle.
True to my word, in a second I was back outside again.

Trading oh yeah, I've heard *Tantilla* with the man who was
    wearing Vons take-out salad bar bags around his feet and
    moving and cussing along with a smile on his face.
He was a liberal arts major from 1966 Vietnam campus.
He said my commencement speaker was agent orange and
    the romanticism I learned was that the government is very
    sexual and don't let nobody tell you different.
    They just want to fuck you.

He said he was 1/6 Sioux, but he felt a little corny telling me
    that the part of him that was Indian was his heart and
    his brain and his spirit was what kept him alive and he said
    I know that shit about every white man thinks his grandma
    is from a popular tribe, but really I am.
He said when he was in grade school, he was the only kid who
    wanted to be an Indian.
Everybody else wanted to be cowboys.

He laughed and said John Cougar Mellencamp was probably
    Francis Scott Key in another life.
Chick, he said, my legal name is Tension.

Suddenly I heard from inside the club Bryan Harvey howling
    "and the righteous and the righteous shall fall" –
    singing for pregnant women and tee-shirted gasoline
    children with Steinbeck novels under their oil streaked cash
    registers.

These were the lullabies that know your stomach like blankets
    you double over you like you had someone to believe in once.
The rowdy blankets with tooth marks kicked off with the
    bedspread and sheets for sliding out windows when night
    time was never dark enough.

Tension said I know you're thinking you want to get to know
    me better, and it may be possible because reunions are
    constantly being held.
The invitations are being printed in Washington and we can
    bring as many guests as we want.
There will be fish, chicken, all-you-can-eat servings, all you have
    to do is be prepared to swallow any food dye that's red,
    white and blue,
        then red again.

God must be getting tired of the stupidity of man.
I bet he's ready to become an atheist.

But young girl who needs me,
I might make you stumble.
I have no telephone.
When I eat, it's potato chips and cigarettes that have already
been used.
When I sleep, it's in the arms of a tree.
When I love someone, I can't tell them.
I'm telling you now.
When I split, I leave 18 cents for a good life.

He handed me a quarter and said,
        'cause I don't know you well enough.

TENT

You remind me of this sheet my mom put on my bed.
It's cool to lay against.
It keeps me warm only when I touch myself
  but it's kind of sexy when I lie still.
This sheet is thin like the word help, fragile when I move.
Instead of moving with me, the sheet tears.

When I kick my legs or spread my arms,
  I make a window for G-d, the air,
  or the ceiling to stay or abandon me
  like a clown making balloon shapes.
This sheet looks like a hyena
  laughter despite loss
  creativity despite injury
  fucking with the one who fucks with all my infinities
  and all my emotional stretch marks
  as I start the night naked
  and wake up wearing clothes.

THERE'S THIS STATION

There's this station that plays the classic rock sound.
One time a D.J. referred to a woman as a dog.
It reminded me of the time I went with the other high schoolers
    to a comedy club and someone on stage heckled me —
    called me a dog.

From my front row seat, visions of the movie *Marty* flashed
    through my mind.

I saw the thimble of water where the ugly duckling swims
    twice as fast as the swan.
Yet, no koi pond allows her entrance.

I heard the angry tickle that sounded like proof
    one-third of the larynx was removed at birth.

From my front row seat, a tear jumped into the laugh track.
The guffaws sounded soggy.
The people who threw their heads back in laughter
    ended up with broken necks.

Every time that station plays Joni Mitchell, Led Zeppelin and
    Creedence Clearwater Revival, I hear growling like a
    subliminal whistle only a misfit hears.

What a world where women come equipped with either
    firm tits or paws.
Yet, when you held me, I felt myself lose the tail that hung
    between my legs like a Pavlovian genital.

Like a ringing in my ears,
    I only just now knew how to answer.

THIS THRILL

Well… August…. lost the old vintage Sprite bottle from
    Cerrillos, New Mexico
And the stones picked up on the road when not picking up sage.
Bingo accidentally threw away these natural souvenirs.
I didn't have my period so it was good to sleep without
    worrying about the red train.
Neal Cassady didn't have to worry about his period when
    he roamed globes.

Heard a lot of John Prine and lovely a cappella versions of
    Leonard Cohen.

August gave me Sasha.
My given at the airport in the Land of Enchantment nickname.
All my compadres nicknamed on nicked faces from shaving away
    L.A. domestic monotony.

Freeways are nothing short of freedom.
The pores of cheekbones oh so open.
Such an open time.

Natan knows she sleeps in nothing but a yellow ribbon.
I sleep in giggles here while others sleep on their backs.
Snoring in the choir.
O Solo Mio.

It's nice the women of the men trusted me.
It's not so nice the women of the men trusted me.

I got horny once in an A&W Root Beer stand.
Probably just cholesterol.

The Cowboy Junkies lobotomized Corky's really good mood ring.
Colorado Springs ran through my fingertips like a gigolo who sees
    over his shoulder the Pope.
I got a bracelet in the iconoclastic colors of red, white and blue,
    given to me in Indian country.

I told Biff I will never cut my wrist – probably.
He said did you hear what Ellyn said?
Breaking the fourth wall of calling me by my nickname.
His blue eyes sort of trembled.

Went to a Safeway.
Bought a health bar and a loaf of bread.
I was Grain Mother, Earth Head.
Maternal instincts when somebody only wanted red meat and
    somebody else only wanted alfalfa sprouts.

Radio Shacks have a shiny feel in Albuquerque.
Retail and malls seem out of place in this pure place.
The airport thinks I'm a movie star.

I laid levitated yet flesh-like from the plane to the home sweet
    motel room at the Regal 8 Inn, there were 7 of us.

The gambler among us trusts numbers in motels and
    letters in Vegas,
but he wouldn't dance with me when the whispers began and
    the cutting in of dance partners started at La Fonda Hotel in
    Santa Fe (owned by Peter Fonda's legs, a biker, and fajita
    blue corn-haired tortilla groupies.)

The Dance in Santa Fe:

Biff the waltz with the baseball stuff under the eyes to keep the
    sun above,

Cooky the square dance,
Rusty the new wave flirt,
Bingo the behind me sway,
Mingo the wow of new history,
Corky the American tourist with a choice.

Back in L.A. the radio keeps playing Janis Ian's song *At Seventeen*.
I bought a postcard of Janis Joplin at Poor Richard's in
      Colorado Springs.
It was a photograph at an early point in her life as though
      Chagall was a cameraman of hootenanny.
It was taken in a moment when it was only her looking at life
      and not life traipsing over her.
She looked peaceful, like fucking acoustic guitars was probably
      the way to an old soul.
You go electric, you go suicide.

Out of habit, I was in an L.A. bookstore.
I looked to see if they had *Zombie Jamboree*.
The book was a momentary theme song for the tour.
Almost everyone works in a bookstore at some point in their life.
I was the baby of the upholstery.
The voice of The Captain & Tennille.

The trip was beautiful!
It was like being ensconced in a kind of Don Henley video.
No airbrush.
No touch-ups.
Just as the skies talked in my simple glee and simple heartbreak.
A movie is really one still at a time, but our eyes chrome-key
      and blend it together so it's motion.
I see it frame by frame.
As the Leonard Cohen song goes, "seems so long ago Nancy
      was alone looking at the late late show through a
      semi-precious stone.

In the house of honesty her father was on trial,
   in the house of mystery there was no one at all."

Does shyness triumph over lips and are lips where it's at anyway?
On the road I didn't wear a hat, but my head was covered.
10-gallon saxophones of yes, you are changing.
Magic carpet rides in old Cadillacs red and white.
Could the colors represent some drag race between cultures as
   they dance around each other in cities and deserts?
Ancient sunlight picks up the peace sign in Biff's car.
The sage on the backseat floor of Bingo's car is giving four
   directions to all the confused tourists who left home
   without it.
Old Cadillacs with the wisdom of old tattoos.
People in restaurants sighed.
Eyewitness to indecision.
Nourishment came.

When I came back to L.A., odometers breathed erotically.
I sat in gridlock.
Smiled with giddy insanity.
For four and a half days everything still seemed possible.
Coming off the trip.
Coming down.
Coming into Los Angeles with nearly the same birthday as
   Arlo Guthrie,
   the mantra should have been written on the wall.
Happiness a chameleon minstrel.
Fleeting reality.
Owies of thousands of miles of imbalanced balanced luggage
   on our heads.
No hope for posture.
No future.
Still the piano bar in my heart is taking requests written in
   chapstick on a napkin.

A medley of freak-out.
I play it like Oscar Levant.
I feel the crescendo.
A wall of walls of sound.

Swimming in Creedence Clearwater Revival.
Without ever clearing the water.
Taking no boats.
Sand gets in my mouth.
All the religions of solitude.
I call (213) KINDRED and get answering machines, roommates,
    dads.
So L.A. – yet so fucking puts me in my place.
Nowhere.
Why can't we all go on together?

The old Indian saying, "I will fight no more forever."
People got lives here.
They are trying to settle in.
I feel like a magician who, instead of levitating the assistant,
    levitated herself for a long while.
I want the high consciousness rush of being the being in a
    Midnight Oil video.
Going everywhere.
Peter Garrett shouts, "Your dream world is just about to end.
Your dream world will fall," (and he almost got a place in
    Parliament in Australia.)

But segue here comes Don Henley and now the other Eagles are
    arguing over royalties in my cheekbones.

I wake up in my room at home in California, feeling like it is the
    cliché lonely motel room in dusty places of Sam Shepard's
    wild eyebrows.
More lonely than when I actually was in those places.

In those rooms.

Many days go by.

Calls to guys don't get returned.

We become a dysfunctional touring family of words.

Tony Bennett sings off key.

I feel sad.

The trip quote unquote ended.

Morning as my ear tilts to the bowl.

That's Jack Kerouac snap crackle popping in my cereal.

My beat appetite.

The whispers of further say continue!

Further is O.K.

I'm committed to you like granola.

Like Dylan bootlegs.

When I see things.

I sure do.

Struggling with those merged classics in my eyes.

Suddenly Last Summer and *Brief Encounter*.

People stop me on the street –
    different from being stopped on the road.
And say congratulations,
    you survived traveling with the Carma Bums.
You should get a purple heart medal.
I think of *Johnny Got His Gun* by Dalton Trumbo.
The nameless protagonist, the only piece of skin he could feel
    was a bit in his neck.
Trumbo, blacklisted during a time in America when
    the nameless were given, screeched names in front of
        House Un-American Activities Committee members.
Mental firing squads.
Blacklisted, he had vision – or was it he saw –
    so he was blacklisted?
The war came in, closed the purple heart around the novel.
The war looked proud.

I say incredulously *I* should get a purple heart – nah.

They look at me and think, wow, chick is touchy and literal.
She must be premenstrual.
They think they were being clever.
It's small talk, good intentioned, coffeehouse something to say
    to somebody stuff.
But I have been getting kicked in the ass and funny bone with
    literal.

I heard you tell me, "I love you."
I can't hide behind amnesia or anything.
The Berlitz Romance language of obvious.
I am the Helen Keller of your fear with no teacher.
Even Van Morrison songs can't at-one me with inner peace.
I'm a ballerina to your paralysis.
You go denial of every sense and every wonder up to the seven.
These are Dostoyevsky songs, angry 'cause he's been asked to
    pay to play.
The Hunchback of Notre Dame has been asked to audition.
Cyrano de Bergerac has a billboard on Sunset.
Little Big Man.
Opening old wounds found in the same place in each of us.
Low self of physical esteem.
I believed in you.
That you wouldn't do it.
There are many fears you could have had instead.
Spiders are popular in Canoga Park.
You might have reacted in the shadow of the queen of diamonds.
The material blonde I'll never be even if I dared touch peroxide
    which might eat way more than my roots.

Time is a human withdrawal/junkie sweat and toy store appetite.
I eat the sunrise.
I sleep through the sunset.

It's more than rejection.
It's like murdering the heat of promise.
Busting the faith.
Does this sort of thing happen to Charles Kuralt a lot?

Almanacs live on my tongue.
I recommend travel if you realize you can't go home again.
Your home changes cities.
Your home is a welcome mat of quicksand.
Your mailbox is shivering.
Your questions are answered in code.
The dance schools won't admit you even with your tap shoes.

But yes, it's worth it.
A loaded parade is always pointed at my head.
But in a parade, the road is covered with shoulders to tap
        and say...

Oh excuse me, I'm lost, come back to me.

TRAIN

It's like when a train is making a stop at a city
    that's never had a train before.
Sometimes you ride with the baggage.

It's like dreaming night after night of *An American In Paris* and
    not knowing if you are Gene Kelly, George Gershwin,
    Leslie Caron, Nina Foch or Oscar Levant,
    or a medley no one will ever score.

It's like being made of apples and finding you're forbidden.

It's like the episode of *Twilight Zone*
    where the bandages are removed
    and you're still appalling.

It's like finding the perfect Mont Blanc pen and
    as soon as you put it in your pocket,
    the world changes to invisible ink.

It's like someone said come out of the cave
    decorated with rare L.P.'s and
    canaries who rebel against the coal miner's broken throat,
    you feel the avalanche in the bone of the land itching like
    the first day of junior high.

It's like someone yodeled to you and when you yodeled back,
    they set fire to your Nelson Eddy and Jeanette McDonald records.

It's like wearing 3D glasses and saying let's be silly together
    and the other person saying G-d, you're ugly.

I trusted you.
    I've worn glasses since I was two.

UNREQUITED

There are as many stages of unrequited love as there are
    theaters on the tip of my tongue
Some seem so remote they make a light year away seem as close
    as a halo and the head of a pin
People don't look for the twilight in my eyes
It's shiver time in thermometer row
I got canker sores from biting my upper lip that laughs at the
    idea it should be stiff
I'm getting used to watching the world pair off like a
    neurotic ark that looks Titanic to me
Yet sometimes I take the ocean and gargle salt and rafts and
    turn it into mermaids who will not be drowned by crashing
    head first into buoys with cactus
    buoys with the swimsuit issue dilating their judgment
Sometimes I feel people have ten pairs of eyes
One for the fashion magazines
One for peer pressure
One for their fathers' expectations
One for their T.V. sets
Five for their hormones
Most need a key to unlock the last eye
But tears will do in a pinch
In that eye music plays around the cornea
    like a harp and retinas dance like a jukebox
It gets real in that eye
Past bravado
Past treason

There treasures fall in the island of ever widening chasm
    between waking up and being able to leave the bed
Life stubs all our toes
Slippers and jammies aren't sufficient

Folklore scratches down our backs
Like sex with the Brothers Grimm
Someone yearned to hold us stories and all
Complicating our tonsils
Wearing lullaby scuba gear
Deserting us in the deep end

We are gymnasts expecting spotters as we cartwheel
    through civilizations
Still chewing on each other's bones

WHEN I WAS IN PARIS

When I was in Paris, I didn't see the Eiffel Tower.
But I guess that means it didn't see me either.

To me, Paris means
Gene Kelly	Oscar Levant
athleticism	breakdowns
dance	cigarettes
genius	brilliance

The little shops for Brie.

The bookstores where James Joyce sat and yakked
    with Samuel Beckett about alphabet soup.

Truffaut, Godard and Rivette sneaking into movies while
    their childhood bedtime stories were read by Balzac.

French poodles and sculptures in the trees.

Stores where meat hangs upside down like bats.

Things are raw.
Things are a bit bloody.

Some people know ten languages and some people sleep
    with pharaoh's eyelids.

A screening of Harry Potter was canceled at a Jewish school.
300 e-mail and 100 phone threats by Lord Voldamart
    impersonators made for less than magical cinema.

It's a hard world for little ones.

There's a sword
There's a swastika
There's a redness in the Seine.

We are living in the Twilight era.

Oh Paris, with your graveyards full of Proust, Colette, Sartre,
    and Morrison,
People look to you. Let my people alone.

I want to see the Eiffel Tower and
I want the Eiffel Tower to see me.

Ellyn Maybe was born in 1964 in Milwaukee, Wisconsin, and moved to Los Angeles in 1980. She lived in New York City from September 1984 till February 1987, and has been back in L.A. since then. Currently, she is an assistant poetry teacher for third grade classes. According to Maybe, "It's really nice, as it's great for the kids to have poetry in their lives so young – they really have imaginative minds and come up with some wonderful metaphors." *Writer's Digest* named her one of "Ten Poets to Watch in the New Millennium". Her work has been included in many anthologies, including *The Outlaw Bible of American Poetry* (Thunder's Mouth) and *American Poetry: The Next Generation* (Carnegie-Mellon University).

Manic D Press Books

The Splinter Factory. Jeffrey McDaniel. $13.95

In the Small of My Backyard. Matt Cook. $13.95

Monster Fashion. Jarret Keene. $13.95

Concrete Dreams: Manic D Press Early Works. Jennifer Joseph, editor. $15

The Civil Disobedience Handbook. James Tracy, editor. $10

This Too Can Be Yours. Beth Lisick. $13.95

Devil Babe's Big Book of Postcards. Isabel Samaras. $11.95

Harmless Medicine. Justin Chin. $13.95

Depending on the Light. Thea Hillman. $13.95

Escape from Houdini Mountain. Pleasant Gehman. $13.95

Poetry Slam: the competitive art of performance poetry. Gary Glazner, ed. $15

I Married An Earthling. Alvin Orloff. $13.95

Cottonmouth Kisses. Clint Catalyst. $12.95

Fear of A Black Marker. Keith Knight. $11.95

Red Wine Moan. Jeri Cain Rossi. $11.95

Dirty Money and other stories. Ayn Imperato. $11.95

Sorry We're Close. J. Tarin Towers. $11.95

Po Man's Child: a novel. Marci Blackman. $12.95

The Underground Guide to Los Angeles. Pleasant Gehman, ed. $14.95

The Underground Guide to San Francisco. Jennifer Joseph, ed. $14.95

Flashbacks and Premonitions. Jon Longhi. $11.95

The Forgiveness Parade. Jeffrey McDaniel. $11.95

The Sofa Surfing Handbook. Juliette Torrez, ed. $11.95

Abolishing Christianity and other short pieces. Jonathan Swift. $11.95

Growing Up Free In America. Bruce Jackson. $11.95

Devil Babe's Big Book of Fun! Isabel Samaras. $11.95

Dances With Sheep. Keith Knight. $11.95

Monkey Girl. Beth Lisick. $11.95

Bite Hard. Justin Chin. $11.95

Next Stop: Troubletown. Lloyd Dangle. $10.95

The Hashish Man and other stories. Lord Dunsany. $11.95

Forty Ouncer. Kurt Zapata. $11.95

The Unsinkable Bambi Lake. Bambi Lake with Alvin Orloff. $11.95

Hell Soup: the collected writings of Sparrow 13 LaughingWand. $8.95

The Ghastly Ones & Other Fiendish Frolics. Richard Sala. $9.95

King of the Roadkills. Bucky Sinister. $9.95

Alibi School. Jeffrey McDaniel. $11.95

Signs of Life: channel-surfing through '90s culture. Joseph, ed. $12.95

Beyond Definition. Blackman & Healey, eds. $10.95

The Rise and Fall of Third Leg. Jon Longhi. $9.95

Specimen Tank. Buzz Callaway. $10.95

The Verdict Is In. edited by Kathi Georges & Jennifer Joseph. $9.95

The Back of a Spoon. Jack Hirschman. $7

Baroque Outhouse/Decapitated Head of a Dog. Randolph Nae. $7

Graveyard Golf and other stories. Vampyre Mike Kassel. $7.95

Bricks and Anchors. Jon Longhi. $8

Greatest Hits. edited by Jennifer Joseph. $7

Lizards Again. David Jewell. $7

The Future Isn't What It Used To Be. Jennifer Joseph. $7

Please add $4 to all orders for postage and handling.

Manic D Press • Box 410804 • San Francisco CA 94141 USA

info@manicdpress.com   www.manicdpress.com